maido

A gaijin's guide to Japanese gestures and culture

Christy Colón Hasegawa

Schiffer Publishing Ltd

4880 Lower Valley Road • Atglen, PA 19310

Library of Congress Control Number: 2016943978

ISBN: 978-0-7643-5267-6
Printed in China

Published by Schiffer Publishing, Ltd.
4880 Lower Valley Road
Atglen, PA 19310
Phone: (610) 593-1777; Fax: (610) 593-2002
E-mail: Info@schifferbooks.com
Web: www.schifferbooks.com

For our complete selection of fine books on this and related subjects, please visit our
website at www.schifferbooks.com. You may also write for a free catalog.

Schiffer Publishing's titles are available at special discounts for bulk purchases
for sales promotions or premiums. Special editions, including personalized covers,
corporate imprints, and excerpts, can be created in large quantities for special
needs. For more information, contact the publisher.

We are always looking for people to write books on new and related subjects. If you
have an idea for a book, please contact us at proposals@schifferbooks.com.

Credits and Acknowledgments

I would like to express my gratitude to all the crazy characters who didn't shy away from the camera and to the many people who helped make this book: Greg, Cristina, Photographer Hal, my folks, Sydni, Jig, Figer, Tiburon, Adriana, Tati, Lola, Ty, Ayano, Hideki, Juan, Carmen, and Comedor Nikkai and the Sid Lee team.

Special thanks to Miwa and David, for being the best hostesses the two weeks I was in Japan for this project. Yuki M. and Aki for being my Nihongo consultants. Erica, for encouraging me all those nights over vino to take the Maido concept out of my head and put it on paper. Without you, this would still only be an idea—domo-domo! And Cora; to be honest, your name should be credited below as an editor, as you took the first complete draft and helped define the tone, bringing consistency to the writing that the book so badly needed. Seriously, is there anything you're NOT amazing at? And last but definitely not least, my "thank yous" would not be complete if I didn't acknowledge my biggest supporter Jurriaan, who kept on me to finish the book. I LOVE you!

- CC

creator, writer, and photography *Christy Colón Hasegawa*

artistic direction and layout *Adrien Sanchez Valero*

contributing writer and humor editor *Geoff Shakespeare*

line editors *Wendy Alexander-Adams and George Powell*

introduction

MAIDO

A *Gaijin's* Guide to Japanese Gestures and Cultures

"Raise your hand in front of your face with your palm directed inwards. Make a fist. Now extend your middle finger."

You know the meaning of this gesture, right? If you are reading this book in a coffee shop, on the bus, or during a weekly catch-up with your boss, you are probably also painfully aware that people don't like to be given "the finger." That's because everyone everywhere knows that raising your middle figure is an action we use to tell everyone else on this planet to kindly go ... piss off. It's a simple, easily learned gesture that's recognized worldwide.

Unfortunately, not all gestures are universal. Unlike emotions, which appear spontaneously on our faces, gestures are learned culture by culture. So while we all make the same "eww" face when we see someone puke on themselves—whether it's in the middle of an open-air market in Marrakech or a state dinner at the White House—gestures are much more dependent on the culture and history of the individuals making them.

If you rely on the gestures you already know to communicate with Japanese people in Japan, you are likely to be misunderstood at best and make a complete ass of yourself at worst.

About the Author

Born and raised in Japan on a US military base by a Japanese mother and a Puerto Rican American father, Christy was fascinated and at times humored by how the gestures her father used didn't always translate over when used with her mom and her Japanese side of the family.

For example, in Japan, the innocent act of pretending to steal a kid's nose won't get smiles and laughs from their onlooking mother; rather, it will be met with a look of disgust. That's because the motion of sticking the tip of the thumb between the index and middle finger in Japan is the gesture for "sex" and, in some regions, "clitoris." Don't get down on yourself if you've already done this; at least you now know why your Japanese host family keeps you away from their kids.

Maido Meaning

Maido (*my-dough*, not to be confused with that childhood favorite, Play-Doh™) describes several of the most common Japanese gestures and defines their meanings and the cultural context that surrounds them. The word **maido** is a slang term commonly used in the Kansai region of Japan (Osaka, Kyoto, and Kobe) and is short for **maido arigatou**, which literally means, "thank you every time." People often use **maido** as a greeting in business and sales, and as a send-off to a business's best customers, as if to say, "come again" or "thank you." In this case, Maido is welcoming you to a world where you don't offend every single Japanese person you meet.

In Maido, you'll see young fashionistas, salarymen, and insane fad starters such as lolitas, yankiis, gyarus, and more demonstrating Japanese gestures. Each photograph depicts the ideal form of a particular gesture and also captures the colorful and absolutely crazy characters running amok in Tokyo and Osaka. As an added bonus, they're pretty awesome to look at, too.

Japanese gestures are a world of their own, much the way the language and the country are.

By learning a few simple gestures you can hopefully avoid making intercultural slip-ups and win the respect of locals. And who knows—maybe the next time you walk into the local **izakaya** (watering hole) you may be lucky enough to hear someone saying, "Maido! Maido!" to you.

Key: How to Make the Most of this Book

To help you find your way around Maido we have created a quick color-coded guide for easy reading. Please review the key below and become familiar with the layout before diving in!

Enjoy!

Picture of the gesture

please and sorry ◀ Name of the gesture in English

Onegaishimasu and *Gomennasai* ◀ Name of the gesture in Japanese
お願いします・ごめんなさい

Bring the palms of both hands together, fingers pointing ◀ How to do the gesture
upward, and bow your head slightly.

This is a multi-use gesture for asking a favor or saying you are sorry. As in any country, ◀ Situations in which the gesture could be used and/or descriptions
"puppy dog eyes" are helpful in achieving the desired result. Or you could try not
screwing things up royally in the first place. But where's the fun in that?

1 - Getting Started

2 - Advanced

3 - Men, Women and Love

4 - Wining & Dining

5 - Slang

6 - Insults

7 - Extras

Getting Started

chapter 1

Watashi
私

Make a fist, palm in, and point your index finger to the tip of your nose.

In most countries, the nose is nothing more than a squishy lump of flesh in the middle of the face. Sure, it's good for smelling and—depending on how poorly you were brought up, picking—but it's nothing special. In Japan, however, the nose is considered the entrance to the tummy, and the tummy is where we believe the spirit dwells. This differs from the belief of people of other cultures who deem the heart the spiritual center of the body. The samurai suicide ritual **seppuku** (better known as **hara kiri**, meaning "belly cutting"—or more causally as "oh my Buddha that dude just totally cut his stomach open!") is based on this belief.

to point

Yubi wo sasu
指を指す

Make a fist and point your index finger to the tip of the other person's nose.

We will point directly at your face to indicate "you." While in other countries this gesture is reserved for jerky waiters, cheating spouses, or anyone else you desperately want to throttle, in Japan it's not offensive at all because the nose is considered a spiritual on ramp. So throw out those useless Anglo manners and point away. Your Japanese friends will be delighted that you know the way to their souls.

please and sorry

Onegaishimasu and Gomennasai
お願いします・ごめんなさい

Bring the palms of both hands together, fingers pointing upwards, and bow your head slightly.

This is a multi-use gesture for asking a favor or saying you are sorry. As in any country, "puppy dog eyes" are helpful in achieving the desired result. Or you could try not screwing things up royally in the first place. But where's the fun in that?

after you

Osakini douzo
お先にどうぞ

Extend your arm and hand in front of your body, palm tilted and facing up.

In Japanese business settings there are precise rules when it comes to even a simple act, such as leaving the room. In most Western countries polite men will wait for women to proceed first, but in Japan the hierarchy of authority dictates who will pass first. Since that hierarchy is still a time- honored tradition, usually the people with the penises get to go first. So don't be surprised if you see a woman holding doors open or slinking over to the buttons in the elevator to allow the big tofu to go first.

Chivalry. What?

excuse me, passing through

Suimasen, mae wo tourimasu
すいません、前を通ります

While slightly bowing your head, stretch one hand away from the body, palm facing sideways at chest level, and move your hand up and down in short strokes when passing in front of someone.

This gesture is used as an apology when passing in front of someone and is similar to saying **sumimasen** (excuse me). In a small nation crowded with 130 million people, you will need to politely pass through crowds. Well, you don't have to pass through politely, but you might as well. Having 130 million Japanese people thinking you're kind of a jerk isn't half as cool as it sounds. This gesture will come in handy as you weave your way through the cramped, narrow streets and back alleys of any major city. If you want a Moses effect, be sure to add a friendly smile.

bowing

Ojigi
おじぎ

Ladies, cup your hands in front of your sacred spot. Gentlemen, place your hands at your sides. From this position, simply bend at the waist and bow with a straight back and eyes looking downward.

Bowing is an essential gesture in Japan for hellos and goodbyes, but it can express just about everything else, too. Bows can mean "excuse me," "thank you," "I'm sorry" or "nice to meet you." Age, gender, company hierarchy, and situation determine bow angle. Bowing is not to be taken lightly. For a Japanese person, not knowing how to bow is like a Westerner not knowing where to go to the bathroom when they visit a friend's house. But don't worry, as a beginner, if someone bows to you, you can't go wrong by bowing slightly longer and at a slightly deeper angle than they do. When in doubt remember BAG (the Bowing Angle Guide).

Bowing Angle Guide (BAG)—don't leave home without it:
- 15° bow is called **eshaku**, and is used for casual greetings or apologies, meaning **konnichiwa** (good afternoon) or **sumimasen** (excuse me). It's the burger and fries of bows. Quick, easy, and it gets the job done.
- 30° bow or **futsu rei** is a formal greeting used when meeting new employees, superiors at work, or public officials. It's the bowing equivalent of an office Christmas party: awkward, stiff, mandatory, and only remotely entertaining if somebody gets totally plastered.
- 45° **Saikei rei**, literally "most respectful bow," is used to convey deep respect or an apology. This is most often used only when you are trying to win a new client, greeting the CEO of your company, or asking for forgiveness because you've accidentally woken up naked in a temple after a late night out.

yes

Hai
はい

Nod your head up and down saying, "hai."

At first glance it may seem this gesture is the same worldwide, but the major difference in Japan is there are times when you would answer with "**hai**" to a negative question rather than "**iie**"
(p. 13).

Example:
"You're not the asshole who ate all the tuna rolls?"

"**Hai**" (I am not that asshole).

no

Iie
いいえ

Shake your head side-to-side when saying "iie."

Phew! This gesture is pretty much the same as everywhere else except India—but that's a different book.

getting someone's attention

Hito no chumoku wo atsumeru
人の注目を集める

Extend your arm and hand and tap someone on the shoulder two or three times with your fingers.

One of the first things you'll notice as a visitor to Japan is the noise. Unless you're way up in the mountains or locked in somebody's soundproof basement, it's almost never quiet. Almost everything you may come across—from traffic signs, convenience store doors, escalators, elevators, to toilets—talks to you. On the plus side, it feels pretty good the first time your bath tells you it's ready for you to get in.

On the negative side, since we are inundated with constant voices from nearly all directions, we are really good at tuning out voices. If you're trying to get our attention by speaking to us, odds are we'll just assume you're a talking "walk" sign. Because of this, grabbing our attention is best done by tapping us on our shoulder instead of speaking.

Obake
おばけ

Make both hands limp and dangle them in front of your body.

The Japanese love scary shit. From their ancient folklore to their modern cinema, they love getting scared to death by a good story. Ghost stories and horror movies are especially popular in the summer because goosebumps are believed to help cool down the body. But no matter what the weather, scary movies are always popular.

Japanese ghost stories are so incredibly freaky they've become the world standard for disturbing horror films. Movies like *The Ring* and *Grudge* have added the image of the disheveled, crook-legged Japanese spirit to the pantheon of classic movie monsters. When we want to depict one of these bone-chilling spooks we simply imitate lifeless hands. With any luck you won't have to use this gesture to describe a real ghost. Or will you?

uh-huh, i hear you

Un-un, kiite imasu
うんうん、聞いています

Nod your head up and down in quick succession once every two to three seconds, and more frequently during a serious discussion. Nodding is almost always done while saying "un-un" (yes-yes) in rhythm with the nods.

This gesture should never be interpreted as meaning "yes." Accustomed to bowing, we will nod our heads when someone is talking to us—even on the phone. This gesture merely means, "I hear you. Uh-huh. Continue," even though we use the same word for "yes."

Be careful when you're discussing serious matters and keep in mind that in business settings, we rarely make decisions on the spot. Many a Western business person has found themselves misinterpreting a potential Japanese client and paying the price later, as have many Western guys at singles' bars.

come over here

Kochi oide
こっちおいで

Palm down, stretch out either arm in front of your body, knuckles first, fingers facing the ground and wave your fingers in unison.

Commonly mistaken by first-time visitors to Japan to mean "sayonara" or "sit down," this Japanese gesture is one of a few that has made its way across oceans to other continents. If you've ever been to an Asian restaurant or market you have most definitely been greeted by the ceramic sculpture of the **Maneki Neko** (beckoning cat). Derived from this Japanese gesture, it's a friendly looking kitty with one paw up, which in some cases beckons mechanically. Besides being unbelievably cute, the **Maneki Neko** is believed to bring the owner of the shop or restaurant good luck.

The meaning changes depending what the **Maneki Neko** is holding or which paw is up:

- Left paw raised: Brings in customers and is best for bars. In Japanese, someone who can really drink is called **hidari-kiki** (left-handed).
- Right paw raised: Brings wealth.
- Both hands raised: This kitty just wants to party down and raise the roof!

This gesture is also used by the non-ceramic cat residents of Japan to indicate we would like you to come toward us. But don't worry, we won't expect you to give us any money—most of the time.

thank you

Arigatou
ありがとう

Place one hand up vertically and perpendicular to your face and do a short, quick karate chop.

Originally a samurai's way of thanking someone with a **katana** (sword), this gesture still exists—with the hand serving as the sword. Why samurai used to thank people by waving their swords in their faces is still a mystery.

Whatever its origins, the gesture is still used today, mostly by men when someone is buying a round of beer. You will also see sumo wrestlers use a similar gesture when accepting their prize money after a winning bout. Rumor has it they also use it to thank the poor soul who has to clean their sweaty loincloths, but unless you are very, very unlucky, you will never have to do that.

wrong

Chigau
違う

With your hands open, cross your forearms as if making a big letter "X" at chest level or in front of your face.

We may say "boo boo" while making this gesture, imitating a wrong-answer game show buzzer. This, along with the **atari** (p. 23) gesture, shows how much we like our crazy, loud game shows. If you're on the street, this gesture can also be used to signal a taxi driver or bus driver there is no need to stop. So can not doing anything, but making a giant "X" with your arms and shouting "boo boo" on the side of a busy street is way, way more fun.

correct

Atari
当たり

Use both arms and make a big circle around your head as if making a big letter "O."

Imagine you're the letter "O" that got kicked out of the Village People. Once you've finished doing that, take off your sailor's outfit, fold it, put it away, and get ready to learn another noise. Like the **chigau** (p. 22) gesture, this one has its own special sound effect. You may hear someone say, "ping-pon" while doing this, imitating a correct-answer ding on those crazy, loud game shows.

Adva

chapter 2

mmm... i'm thinking

Kangae chu
考え中

Cross your arms in front of your chest.

Imagine asking your Japanese friend to dress up like a clown and lift weights while you throw soggy buns at him. Immediately, he crosses his arms and plants a serious look on his face. In the West, you'd be forgiven for thinking you'd crossed the line. Well, what did you expect? Does anybody ever say "yes" to bizarre requests like that? To the Western eye, crossing your arms implies being upset or angry, but in Japan it implies deep contemplation, a la Rodin's *The Thinker*. So don't worry, he doesn't think you're a weirdo with a wet bread fetish—well, he does, but he's just thinking of the best way to tell you.

to laugh

Warau
笑う

Turn your palm toward your face and cover your mouth with your hand.

In Japan, it's common to see a woman covering her mouth when laughing. The most probable reason is that in the old days it was customary for married women to paint their teeth black so they hid them. Why our ancestors went to all the trouble of painting their teeth black just so they could hide them when they laughed is another story. Perhaps ancient Japan wasn't a very funny place.

i don't know

Wakaranai
分からない

With one or both hands upright, palm(s) facing away from your body, and your thumb pointing to your face, shake your hand and head side-to-side. Most often this gesture is done while shaking the head and hand(s) in opposite directions.

During one point in your visit to Japan you may get lost and—if you are not a male visitor—ask for directions. We are known for being polite people, and if we feel like we can't properly explain the directions, we might be inclined to walk you to your destination. On the other hand, if we make this gesture and you note the hand shaking speeds up or is accompanied by an occasional grunt, you've become a nuisance and it's time to find someone else who might do the walk with you.

i get it!

Naruhodo
なるほど!

Position one hand palm up. With the other hand make a fist and hit your open palm.

Similar to slapping yourself in the forehead when you finally get it, we go for the less abusive but equally clear way of letting you know that you've gotten through. It's not as fun as watching someone hit themselves in the head, but it is a little safer.

hot

Atsui
あつい

Lightly pinch your earlobe between your thumb and index finger.

The next time you touch something hot and there's no cold water in sight, do what we do: go for the earlobes. The earlobes are the coolest body part, so it makes a crazy kind of sense. Well, if you're a guy your scrotum is cooler than the rest of your body, too, but we really don't want to see you grabbing your balls every time you pick up a cup of hot tea.

In Japan, you may see a mother tugging her son's earlobes. This should not be mistaken for the **atsui** gesture. In a country where fat earlobes are a symbol of wealth, a little tug never hurt. Men, unfortunately that same rule very much does not apply to any other parts of your body you may be inclined to tug.

calm down

Ochi tsuite
落ち着いて

With both palms facing the ground, move your hands up and down while saying, "Maaa. Maaa. Maaa."

Although most in the West have an image of us as serene and Zen calm, there are times when we get pissed off. Whether the local supermarket is out of our favorite brand of fermented soy beans or a particularly tough final boss cannot be beat in Super Mario Bros.™, we sometimes get mad.

If you are witness to someone blowing their stack, this gesture can be used to try to calm them down.

something stinks

Nanka kusai
なんか臭い

Wave your hand in front of your face and/or pinch your nose with your index finger and thumb.

Japan has its share of beautiful scenery. From its pristine mountain tops to the simple elegance of countryside temples, the sights in Japan rival those anywhere in the world. It also has its share of smells. Some good—like the delicious odors wafting from the front of a **yakiniku** (grilled meat) restaurant—and some not so good, like the pockets of foul stench coming up from the sewer during the summer.

Like folks elsewhere in the world, we have a simple gesture to warn others that the air around us reeks of rotten eggs. Instead of flat-out saying **kusai** ("P-U"), we make the same gesture we would use to fan away or block the smell from being breathed in. As an added bonus, the hand movements actually help wave some of the offending air away.

this way please

Kochira e dohzo
こちらへどぞ

Fully extend your arm and point your hand in the direction a person should go while tilting your head in the same direction.

At restaurants, and in just about every other setting, you will quickly notice the exceptionally high level of customer service. Royalty treatment is the norm. From the dirty hole-in-the-wall bar to high-end joints, this gesture will be used to show guests to their table.

In the last few years we have taken the "royalty treatment" to new heights. Amongst salarymen, there is a growing popularity of Maid Cafés, where customers can live out a twisted fantasy as a rich European. Waitresses are dressed in little French maid costumes and greet each individual with "welcome home master" as they come through the door. If the specialty treatment isn't enticing enough, did I mention most places have dark reflective flooring? Why else would all the **hentais** (perverts) go to a café and pay close to double the normal price for a cup of brewed coffee?

how embarrassing

Tereruna
照れるなー

Tilt your head slightly to one side and scratch it. This gesture is usually accompanied with a smile or giggle.

If you ask someone on the street the name of the person on the ¥5,000 bill and he cocks his head and begins scratching, it's not indicative of head lice ... he's embarrassed because he doesn't have a clue who it is.

FYI, the answer is Inazo Nitobe (1862–1933), a Meiji-era educator. You can use that trick to impress your Japanese friends.

i'm such an idiot

Baka da na
ばかだな

Make a fist and hit your temple lightly with your knuckles two or three times.

If you've done something **baka** (stupid) and you're sure you'll receive a **bakatare** (p. 94) chop to the head, you can always beat the other person to the punch with this gesture. Usually seen in **mangas** (comics) combined with a wink and protruding tongue, this gesture is used to refer to yourself, and it may come in handy when you violate a rule or convention. Maybe a good knock on the side of the head is necessary to confirm that there are noodles inside the ol' noggin.

may i interrupt?

Chotto ii desuka
ちょっといいですか?

At chest level extend your arm, hand facing away from your body, and move that hand forward as if giving someone a high-five repeatedly.

Unlike persons in other places around the world where interrupting is an art form, we're really, really hesitant to butt in when someone else is talking. We're such a bunch of weirdos! Nevertheless, there are occasions where one does need to get a word in, and that's where this gesture comes in. Amid conversation we use this gesture to avoid interrupting too blatantly.

Sono hanashi wa oitoite
その話はおいといて

Hold an imaginary box that is about 8–10 inches long between your hands, then move it a few inches to one side.

In Japan, instead of coming out and saying so, when we want to change the subject we will use this gesture to say, "We have discussed it already. Let's put that subject aside." This is perfect to use when your friend enters the fourth hour of his monologue about his lifelong love of soft jazz or your coworker wants to discuss "synergy" again.

let's not discuss that here

Kokode hanasunowo yamemashyou
ここで話すのを止めましょう

Press your index finger against your lips.

When it's time to keep your lips closed because prying ears might be listening, press your fingers to your lips and say, as the Japanese would, "Shii!"

that sounds like BS

Inchiki kusai
いんちき臭い

Exaggerate the act of sniffing the air. For best results, place your hands at your waist or cross your arms and narrow your eyes.

Not to be confused with **nanka kusai** (something stinks, p. 34), this gesture is used to indicate figuratively bad smells...specifically the kind that come directly from a bull's ass. When someone is distorting the truth, let them know their story is full of you know what.

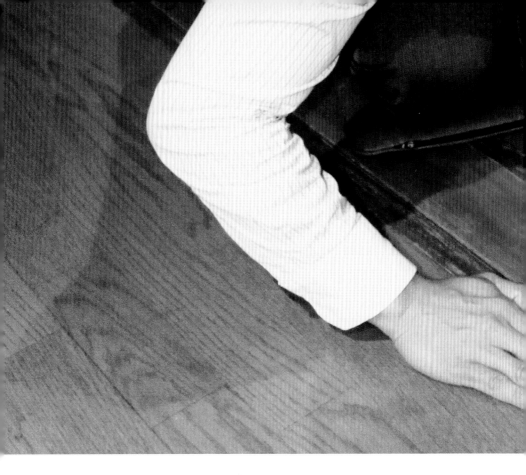

i'm soooo sorry

Dogeza
土下座

Kneel on the ground with your upper body bent over your knees, head bowed to the floor.

This gesture is used in the event of irreparable damage. If **hara kiri** (see p. 3) is the only way to regain honor but disemboweling yourself is going to put a crimp in your weekend, opt for this far less bloody form of apology. The key to this bow is remaining in a bent over position for a few minutes while keeping your nose as close as possible to the ground until the person you are asking forgiveness of is satisfied and gives you permission to look up.

Dogeza is often seen on the six o'clock news when a public apology is necessary. Picture the president of a manufacturing company caught using expired ingredients to make cookies or a politician caught with his pants down and you have the idea. OK, you can stop picturing the pants-less politician now.

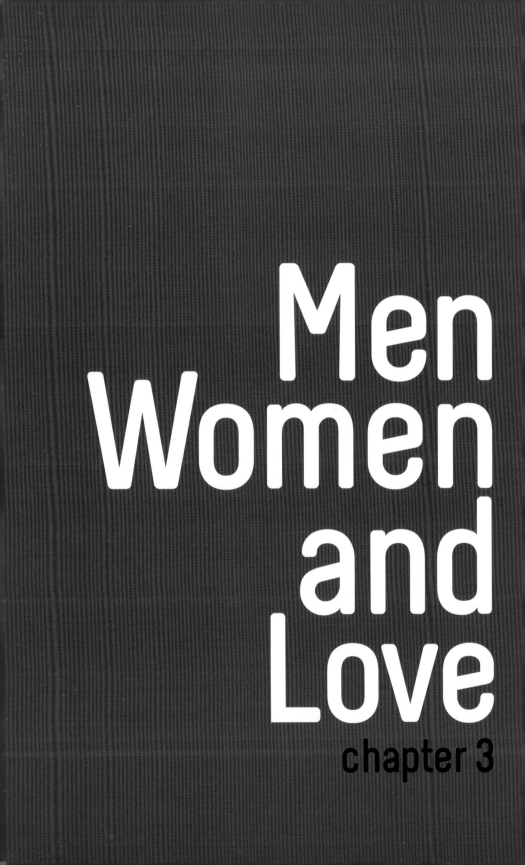

Men
Women
and
Love

chapter 3

condom

Condomu
コンドーム

Form a circle with your index finger and thumb and extend the remaining fingers up.

This familiar Western gesture that is used nowadays in Japan to mean "OK," also refers to condoms. This easy-to-remember gesture should make any late-night condom run in Japan swift and speedy!

man and boyfriend

Otoko and Kareshi
男・彼氏

Make a fist and point your thumb upright.

This gesture can be used to refer to any man, but usually a lover. If those around you suspect the man they saw you with is your "boy toy" and you can't deny it, smile, give them an enthusiastic thumbs up, and go get him, cougar! This gesture can have a slightly negative connotation, as it is mostly used to imply a secret affair. It can also cause a lot of confusion if you forget the Japanese meaning and give someone's grandpa a thumbs up.

woman and girlfriend

Jyosei and Kanojyou
女性・彼女

Make a fist and point your pinkie upright.

Although this gesture generally means woman, the majority of the time it is used to imply a mistress and not just a female friend. When the Japanese want more information about the woman they saw you with, they make this gesture and discreetly ask... **Kore de sho**? ("This, right?")

If it's your wife or girlfriend who sees you getting cozy with a strange woman, she'll make a slightly different gesture involving her fist and your face.

sex

Sekusu
セックス

Stick the tip of the thumb between the index and middle finger.

This gesture alludes to the clitoris or the act of having sex and, in some regions, the penis as well. It makes sense to have a gesture for sex that's more subtle than grunting and thrusting your hips back and forth, but why we have a gesture to refer to such a specific part of a woman's anatomy is unknown. Regardless of where you are in Japan, the gesture is obviously considered obscene, so think twice before trying the old "I got your nose" trick.

pregnant

Ninshin
にんしん

Make an imaginary hump over your stomach as if rubbing a big belly.

This is pretty straightforward: when there is a bun in the oven the belly will bulge. You can also use it to indicate someone has a nice, round Buddha-like belly and needs to cut down on the sweets, but that isn't very nice, is it?

gay and lesbian

Okama and Onabe
おかま・おなべ

Arch your hand backwards, palms out, as if trying to make the letter "C" and touch the opposite cheek with your index finger.

This gesture imitates talking behind someone's back.

There is a large and healthy gay subculture in Japan, but it is very hidden. In a country where homosexuality is not widely accepted, most Japanese gays and lesbians want to keep their activities on the down low. Ni-chome—an area in the Tokyo neighborhood Shinjuku—is Japan's biggest gay district, but it's so discreet that unless you know what you're looking for, you may never see it. Though there are over 300 gay bars, clubs, saunas, massage parlors, and book stores crammed into a tiny three-block radius, the unsuspecting can walk through and have absolutely no idea of the sweet, sinful pleasures happening all around them. Also be warned that if you want to join the party choose your bar carefully, as many don't allow foreign customers.

Wining & Dining

chapter 4

money

Okane
おかね

Form a circle with the index finger and thumb and extend the remaining fingers parallel to the ground.

This "om"-ish gesture means money. No one knows exactly why the gestures for **okane** and condom (p. 51) are so close, but I'm sure this makes prostitution a snap!

wanna

grab a bite?

Tabe ni ikanai
食べに行かない？

With one hand, mime holding a small bowl. With the other, use two fingers as chopsticks and motion with them toward your mouth two or three times.

If you've ever seen someone eating rice out of a bowl, this one is self-explanatory. If someone makes this gesture, he either wants to know if you want to eat or he wants to grab a bite. If you have only one free hand you can go for the modified version and make the chopstick motion sans bowl. If both your hands are occupied you can just go ahead and ask them.

i'm ready to eat and thank you for the meal

Itadakimasu and Gochisousamadeshita
いただきます・ごちそうさまでした

Take both hands and place the palms together, then bow your head oh-so-slightly while saying itadakimasu (before you start eating) or gochisousamadeshita (when you've finished).

Itadakimasu, which means, "I'm ready to eat," should be said while the chopsticks are still on the table.

At the end of the meal, a slight nod of the head accompanied by **gochisousama-deshita** is a nice way of giving praise to the chef for the great eats.

It's important to note that although you may see these gestures being used on one of a million TV cooking shows, they should never be used in a formal dinner setting. Imagine yourself at the Four Seasons proclaiming, "Rub a dub dub! Thanks for the grub." Your Japanese date might find it cute, but your co-workers will think you're a **baka gaijin** (ridiculous foreigner).

sushi

Sushi
寿司

Make a fist with your right hand and extend your index and middle fingers. Use these fingers to tap the palm of your left hand lightly.

This gesture resembles a sushi chef making **nigiri**—sushi rice that is pressed into an oval with some kind of topping over it, usually some kind of fish. It should be noted this gesture can NOT be used interchangeably with **tabeni ikanai** (p. 60). This gesture is much more specific and indicates SUSHI is on the menu for the evening. If you want to request some other kind of food you're out of luck. Unless you have a voicebox. Then you're cool.

wet towel, ashtray, and check, please!

Oshibori, Haizara, and Okaikei onegaishimasu
お絞り・灰皿・お会計お願いします！

Oshibori: Make a motion as if wringing out a towel.
Haizara: Make a letter "O" using both hands.
Okaike: Make a small letter "X" with the index fingers of both hands.

In the big cities of Japan, you may feel as if there is only one speed: fast-forward. Everywhere you look people are racing around like coked-up monkeys as they travel from job to play to home in a never-ending cycle. This hurry-up-and-hurry-up-some-more attitude even extends to basic acts like eating. In Japan, being able to wolf down an entire plate of food in under a minute is seen as a valuable skill. Time equals money in Japan, and there's no profit to be made taking a long lunch. Every second counts!

At restaurants, flash the waiter one of these useful gestures and you will save him the ten seconds it would take to call him over and actually ask for what you want and you'll be swept back into the buzzing and beeping maelstrom that much faster.

how about a drink?

Ippai doh
一杯どう？

Form the letter "C" with your index finger and thumb and tilt your hand as if taking a sip from a sake cup.

After a long day of work, this gesture is unmistakable for "let's go for a drink or two"—or ten. With Western influence, variations of this gesture have popped up. If you want a glass of beer, enlarge your imaginary cup. Just as a side note, when doing this gesture make sure you don't close your index finger and thumb; otherwise, your coworker may suspect you'd rather perform sexual favors instead of having a friendly beer. Not that there's anything wrong with that. Hell, maybe he'd really appreciate that after a hard day's work. Use your discretion.

just a little bit

Chotto dake
ちょっとだけ

Make a fist and extend only your index finger and thumb.

If you're ready to head home from a hard day's work and the big tofu (we don't eat a lot of cheese in Japan) insists on a drink at the local **izakaya** (watering hole) before parting ways, do the old boy a favor and have a drink. Since Japanese workers are expected to drink whenever their boss asks them to, you'll be doing yourself a favor, too. Just make it clear that it's cool only if it's **chotto dake**.

chapter 5

ng

Udega ii
腕が良い

Hit your forearm with your hand lightly.

Unlike most arcades around the world, Japanese game centers (as they are called) have games for all ages and tastes. Even better, they have music games designed for two or more players. This leads to a lot of laughs as you and your friends try to drum or dance your way through the latest J-pop hit. Unfortunately, it also sometimes leads to dance competitions with strangers. If a bystander flashes the **udega ii** gesture before you step up to the Dance Dance Nation™ platform, he's not flipping you the bird. You have just been forewarned...your rival has Usher with milk for breakfast!

what the hell?!

Nandeyanen
なんでやねん?!

Open your hand, fingers extended, and hit someone in the chest or belly with the back of your hand.

If you watch **owarai** (comedy) shows on TV, you will quickly see that **manzai** (Japanese comedy duo) groups don't deny themselves the sublime pleasure of whacking someone when given the chance—especially in response to a nitwitted, idiotic, or dunce remark. The Kansai **manzai** and the **tsukomi** (straight man) are known for their favorite gesture—constantly whacking the **boke** (funny man) in the gut and uttering **Nandeyanen**?!

life is good.
no complaints here.

Hidari uchiwa
左うちわ

With the left hand, pretend as if you are fanning yourself with a fan.

The Japanese fan themselves with the left hand to let people know they can live without worries—or more specifically, they're loaded. Why the left hand, you ask? Well, in the days of samurais and ninjas, it was common to keep the right hand free to grab the sword. With only the **hidari** (left) hand free for the **uchiwa** (fan), it became a gesture meaning "be ready for the unexpected," which in time evolved to mean you have reserves and could live without worry.

This gesture has the added bonus of letting people know you're a colossal jerk who likes to rub his or her wealth in the face of whomever you happen to be with. So why not kill that image and buy the first round?

fired

Kubi
首

Slide your index finger or hand horizontally across your neck as if you are drawing an imaginary line.

Although things have changed slightly as Japan stumbles through years of economic decline, most companies hire their workers for life. Once someone finds a job, they can be pretty certain that unless they screw up badly enough to be mentioned in the local newspaper, odds are they can ride the position to the grave. But in the very rare event they do cock something up so monumentally that they must be canned, their coworkers might give them this gesture. **Kubi** literally means "neck," as in what you need to protect because someone at work is after your jugular and is looking to give you the axe.

arrested

Taiho
逮捕

Cross your wrists or put them together as if they were handcuffed.

Take him away, boys!

This gesture means someone is headed to the can. Just pray you aren't the person being referred to, because despite Japan's modern reputation as a peaceful society of harmless anime freaks, Japanese prisons are among the toughest in the world. Convicts are expected to live lives of extreme austerity. Their heads are shaven, they are allowed only minimal contact with the outside world, and they spend the majority of their days sitting in tiny cells with nothing to do but make imaginary friends to beat the boredom. Most horrible of all, they have to survive on a punishing diet of mostly vegetables and rice! If that doesn't scare you straight, nothing will.

that's difficult to believe

Mayu tsuba
眉唾

Pretend to lick your index finger and run it across your eyebrow.

There is an old Japanese belief that **tanukis** (raccoon-like animals common in Japan) transformed themselves into humans and caused mischief. Everything about them was said to morph except for their eyebrows, which remained wild and bushy. Taming the wild brows with saliva was said to be the **tanukis**' chosen method of remaining incognito. Why they didn't just invest in a pair of tweezers no one knows.

So the next time someone tells a tall tale, show them you're onto them and their bushy brows. Legend also holds that **tanukis** had scrotums so large they could double as parachutes. Unfortunately, there's no gesture based on that, but feel free to make up your own.

paid under the table

Sode no shita
袖の下

Make a motion as if slipping money into the sleeve of a kimono.

Sometimes deals need to be made away from the prying eyes of the public. Whether you're a **yakuza** (p. 91) looking for a leg up on a public construction bid or a creep looking to get a working girl's leg up, shady deals require discretion. The gesture has its origins in the ancient tradition of using kimono sleeves as makeshift pockets—perfect for payments that needed to be made on the sly.

shoplifter

Manbiki
万引き

Make a fist and extend your index finger upright and hooked.

For the most part, theft isn't something you have to worry about too much in Japan. First-time visitors will be amazed at how trusting people are with their possessions. In restaurants, people may actually use their bags to hold seats while they wander out of sight to use the bathroom or order. People even leave their cars running when they pop into a convenience store. Nevertheless, there are sticky fingers in Japan. Use this gesture to tell your friends that a person likes to take what doesn't belong to them. A crooked finger for a crooked person. Easy, right?

Okanmuri
おかんむり

Place both index fingers on the side of your head like horns.

The horns should not be mistaken to mean infidelity as in most Latin cultures—or devil worship as in most heavy metal cultures. This is only done when referring to a third party being angry. For example, if you walk in late to work and your co-worker flashes you the horns, your boss is pissed. Depending how late you are, you may want to review BAG (**ojigi**, p. 10) before paying a visit to his office.

bribe

Wairo
賄賂

Make a motion as if you're slipping imaginary bills into the inside pocket of a suit jacket.

Even though Japan signed the Anti-Corruption Convention in 1999, little has been done to get people back on the straight and narrow. To give you an example of how corrupt some Japanese can be, over 90% of the rivers and streams in Japan have man-made dams. Only about 5% of them really needed a dam, but when government bureaucrats and construction companies get together, the bills that get slipped into the inside pockets aren't always imaginary. The world over, people know that every man has his price. We didn't invent bribery, but we do have one of the coolest hand gestures for it.

bad blood

Naka warui
なか悪い

Repeatedly hit two crossed index fingers together.

When we want to be discreet about a squabble between folks we mime sword fighting with our fingers. You would think the fact that everyone knows what the gesture means would not make it very discreet, but in Japan the appearance of discretion is what's important.

japanese gangster

Yakuza
ヤクザ

Draw a diagonal line on your cheek from ear to mouth with your index finger.

The imaginary line symbolizes a bad-ass gangster knife scar. But be warned, as cool as doing this gesture may make you feel, it should be used with discretion. Like most gangsters, **yakuzas** are a little sensitive about being identified in public, especially by some smart-ass tourist. If a real **yakuza** happens to see you giving yourself one of these imaginary scars, he might take offense and give you a not-so-imaginary one. There are probably a lot of better souvenirs you can bring back from Japan to remember your visit.

Insults

chapter 6

cheapskate

Kechinbo
けちんぼ

Make a fist with your right hand and wave it back and forth in the air.

While you may feel nervous making a fist and moving it in a fashion that may be perceived as a little sexual in nature, relax. It just means the person you're referring to is tightfisted.

stupid!

Bakatare
ばかたれ!

Give a light karate chop with either hand to someone's head.

Blame it on the influence of Ninjas, but when someone does something stupid, children and adults alike will give their friends a karate chop to the head and scream **Baka** (dingbat, jackass, idiot!)! The strength of the chop and the volume of the scream are completely up to you. You can give the offending **bakatare** a light tap if he forgets the sugar in your coffee or really wallop him if he spills it all over your new cashmere sweater. A good gauge is the dumber the act, the firmer the chop—within reason of course.

crazy

Kuru-kuru-pah
くるくるぱー

*With your index finger,
point to your temple and
make two small circles, then
open your hand, palm up.*

When someone has done something
foolish, this simple but effective
gesture will get the message across
that he's loco, crazy, nutty, crackers,
bananas, or has a screw loose. There
may be a few times when you get to
use this gesture to describe someone
else, but as a stranger to the millions
of subtle societal rules and codes
created over thousands of years
of tradition, odds are much better
that somebody will single you out as
cuckoo.

brown-nosing

Goma suri
ゴマすり

Make a fist with one hand and make small circular motion—as if grinding something with a pestle—on the palm of your other hand.

It may come as a surprise, but not everyone has the best of intentions when they're saying something nice about you.

Have you ever been in a situation where someone tells you out of the blue how much he likes your hair, even though you'd barely combed it that morning? For a second you start to feel really good about yourself, then BANG! He's asking you to help him with his move this weekend. When someone starts to excessively flatter you and it's apparent that they wants something more than to make you feel special, make the motion of grinding sesame seeds (**goma suri** in Japanese). This will let them know that although they say they have no hidden agenda when they spend thirty minutes complimenting you on your eyebrows, you know otherwise.

full of it

Hora banashi
ほら話し

Open and close your hand in front of your mouth, pushing your hand forward as you open it.

If someone starts laying it on thick and you know there is nothing to back it up, let them know there's a lot of hot air coming out their trap. This gesture works great if the blowhard you meet at the bar does the **hidari uchiwa** (p. 78) gesture and brags about how much money he's got and you know damn well he doesn't.

arrogant

Tengu ni naru
てんぐに成る

*Make a fist in front of your face and then move it away
from your face as if suggesting a growing nose.*

A clenched fist in front of the face looks similar to the long nose of the arrogant spirits of **tengu** folklore. Known for their pride and vanity, **tengu** traveled the land terrorizing the pious and tricking people into eating dung. Because of this friendly image, the Japanese began using the expression **tengu ni naru** (he is turning into tengu) to describe a conceited person.

There's also a possibility this gesture is in reference to the Europeans who occupied Japan during the Edo period and American forces after WWII, since they were viewed as having big noses and being impossibly arrogant. The exact etymology of this gesture is unclear, but it can easily be used to describe people who think they crap chocolate ice cream.

you're asking for a lickin'

Nagutte yaroh ka
殴ってやろうか

Make a fist and breathe hard on it as if warming it up.

Often used as a playful gesture among children. This is a good way to let a snotty kid know you're warming up your knuckles for a good knock on the head. It's also a good way to let his mother and father know they've failed as parents.

Many foreigners who come to Japan end up as teachers. Bright-eyed and full of hope, these teachers greet their students on the first day of class, ready for a life-altering educational experience. Then some little snot jabs his fingers in the teacher's crack. Known as a **kancho**, this gesture is popular with little boys, and they love to welcome new teachers with it. Show them you won't be pushed around by breathing on your knuckles, and never, ever turn your back on a ten-year-old Japanese kid.

nani nani boo boo

Akanbe
あかんべー

Pull down the skin under your eye and stick out your tongue.

As the Japanese version of the evil eye, this is what kids usually say and do to tease other kids or, in the case of young boys, profess their undying love for the pretty girl who sits across from them in class. It's just as effective as the **nagutte yaroh ka** (p. 102) fist blowing, but it has less implied violence. If you get into trouble with a kid, the choice is yours: threaten them with violence or throw them an evil eye. Either one works, and they're both fun-as-hell ways to scare small, defenseless children!

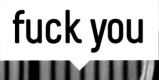

fuck you

Fakku Yuu
ファック　ユウー

Raise your hand in front of your face, palm facing inward.
Make a fist. Now extend your middle finger.

The bird has landed!

Most Japanese don't understand the level of vulgarity that flipping the bird carries elsewhere in the world. This can lead to some shocking moments when young kids might harmlessly give you the finger for no good reason. They may, to the contrary, understand exactly what they're doing and have every good reason to finger you. In that case, fakku yuu, too!

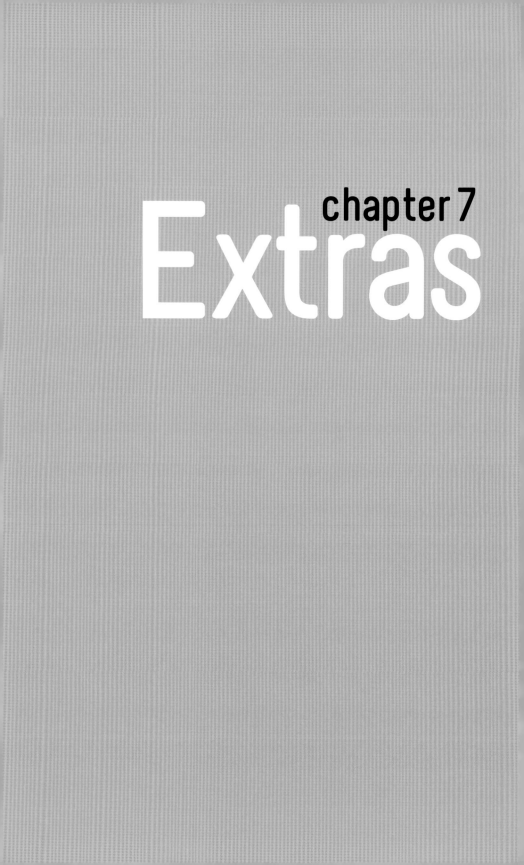

chapter 7
Extras

kneeling

Seiza
正座

Sit on your knees with your legs tucked under your thighs while resting your buttocks on your heels.

Seiza, literally translated as "proper sitting," is an essential part of most traditional Japanese events or arts that require you to sit on tatami, such as tea ceremony, praying, and martial arts.

WARNING: If you're not used to this position, your legs will go numb. Pinching your toes or shifting your weight from left to right will NOT reduce the pins-and-needles sensation. If you plan to spend any length of time in Japan, you will have to get used to having tingly legs.

counting

Kazoeru
数える

We begin counting with our fingers extended and then close them into a fist, starting with the thumb. Once we have reached five, we will raise the pinky finger for six and continue until the hand is open again to reach ten. This may not be all that useful, as you can still count on your fingers however you like and people will get it, but knowing the Japanese way will help you understand when your dinner companions start doing the hand jive while they're sorting out the bill.

pinky promise

Yubikiri
指きり

Intertwine your pinky finger with someone else's pinky finger while singing the Yubikiri song.

Yubikiri lets another person know that you're giving them your word that something will be done. Although it seems pretty cutesy and harmless, be careful before locking pinkies. The cute little song you sing promises not only that you will cut off your pinky if you break the deal, but also that you will drink 1,000 needles.

It's said that the rhyme refers to the timeless punishment of cutting off a finger if you fail to keep a promise—a ritual still practiced by the **yakuza** (p. 91)—and the needles allude to eating the venomous **fugu** (pufferfish). Ouch!

Yubi kiri genman	Pinky Promise
Uso tsuitara	If you're lying
Hari sen bon nomasu	I will make you drink 1,000 needles
Yubi kitta!	And cut your pinky!

peace sign

Peasu
ピース

With your palm facing outward, make a fist and use your index and middle fingers to form the letter "V."

The true origin of this symbol is shrouded in mystery, but what we do know is it was originally employed by Churchill during World War II as a sign of "victory." Its use has been popularized the world over by Japanese tourists who aren't afraid to make the "V" sign in every photo they pose for. Well, what better way to celebrate the fact that you've successfully had your picture taken than with a gesture that once represented the victory of freedom over tyranny? The "V" sign is so common in pictures in Japan that most kids literally master it before they can talk.

In the last few years, a couple variations of the sign have become popular with the younger crowd: school girls will hold up two "V" signs very close to either side of their face (which is said to make the jaw line look thinner); and by far the most "interesting" variation is the combination peace sign with the tongue sticking through. Sexy!

cross-legged

Agura
あぐら

Sit on your buttocks with your lower legs crossed at the ankles or calves with both ankles on the floor. You may tuck your feet under your knees or calves.

Sitting cross-legged is considered informal. Once you have hit your limit with **seiza** (p. 110) style and you're convinced your legs are going to fall off any minute, shifting to **agura** is considered okay if you're elderly with inflamed joints or a non-Japanese guy. If you're still numb after that, well, you're on your own and may consider seeing a doctor.

Ladies, unfortunately, sitting cross-legged is considered rude, so even if you've lost all sensation from the knees down and your toes are bright blue— suck it up!

rock-paper-scissors

Jan-Ken
じゃんけん

Chanting "Jan, Ken, Pon," on pon, players make one of the three shapes with their fist:

Goo (Rock): Fist

Pah (Paper): Hand open

Choki (Scissors) : Make a fist and extend the index and middle fingers

Everyone knows the basic rules of Rock-Paper-Scissors: scissors cut paper, paper covers rock, and rock breaks scissors. Somewhat similar to "Eeny-Meeny-Miney-Moe," this children's game is used for figuring out who gets first dibs or for randomly selecting a person for a group or games. In school yards across the country, thousands of kids use it to decide matters big and small, but in Japan, Rock-Paper-Scissors is also used by grown ups. It's perfect for deciding who has to stay late at the office, who's going to tell the boss you lost the account or, most importantly, who is going to get that last **onigiri** (rice ball).

hip-hip hooray!

Banzai
万歳！

Raise both arms above your head three times while simultaneously shouting "banzai." Usually repeated two or three times.

Not to be mistaken for those wicked miniature bonsai trees, **banzai** is an exclamation meaning, "May you live ten thousand years!" Once used as a battle cry by suicidal soldiers making a desperate, doomed, last-ditch assault on enemy forces, this cheer is now commonly used at the end-of-the-year party at work, weddings, and at the end of a sporting event to express good fortune.

If you ever wanted proof of how definitively we have put our samurai warrior past behind us this gesture should be enough. We've taken one of the most fearsome expressions in the language and turned it into something people say at parties.

That's progress!

bye-bye

Sayonara
さようなら

With your arm extended and palm out, wave your hand from left to right at a speed of about two reps per second.

This is pretty much the same gesture that's used all over the world, but the Japanese also have an upgraded version. Among children and high school students, you will usually see friends saying good-bye with a two-handed wave. Apparently, the one-handed wave doesn't quite convey the same **sayonara** feeling.

wrapping things up with a Tejime

Tejime
手締め

Extend your arms, palms up, rhythmically clapping your hands.

At the end of a special event or even a night of pure unadulterated debauchery we will rhythmically clap hands to end the evening on an upbeat note. The head cheerleader—usually the head honcho or the guest of honor—will prep the squad by yelling **ote wo haishaku** ("lend me your hands"). The cheering squad will take their positions by extending their arms palms up, waiting for the captain to choose one of these three cheers:

Itcho-jime: One clap cheer
Ippon-jime: Three sets of three claps and one final clap cheer (3-3-3-1)
Sanbon-jime: Three sets of the **ippon-jime** cheer (3-3-3-1, 3-3-3-1, 3-3-3-1)

The complete cheer usually goes something like this:

Ote wo hishaku.	Lend me your hands.
Saigou wa <u>sanbon-jime</u> de owarimasu!	We will end with a **<u>sanbon-jime</u>**!
YOH~ (followed by claps)	YOH~ (followed by claps)

* You can replace the cheer (underlined above) with another.

It's the perfect way to cap off an event and reinforce the solidarity of the group, especially if half an hour earlier they were all singing "Dancing Queen" with their neckties tied around their heads. If you are ever oh-so-lucky enough to lead this cheer and you don't know which to close the evening with, a good rule of thumb is the less rhythmic the group the better it is to choose a cheer with fewer claps.

And with that, we too would like to end the book with an **Itcho-jime**.
YOH~

The book has come about as a Sid
Lee Collective initiative—a formalized
program giving the employees of
international ad agency Sid Lee a
chance to realize their personal creative
projects by financing and showcasing
them.

Sid Lee is a creative services firm with
550 professionals working globally from
offices in Montreal, Toronto, New York,
Paris, and Amsterdam. The company
creates transformative consumer
experiences for brands across all contact
points, leveraging true interdisciplinary
collaboration. Rooted in strategic
thinking, Sid Lee offers what they call
commercial creativity services in the
fields of branding, digital and social
marketing, advertising, analytics,
architecture and retail design, and
branded content and entertainment.

Cover design by Adrien Sanchez Valero